He Took a Cab

Also by Mather Schneider

Drought Resistant Strain, Interior Noise Press, 2010

He Took a Cab

Mather Schneider

The New York Quarterly Foundation, Inc.
New York, New York

NYQ Books™ is an imprint of The New York Quarterly Foundation, Inc.

The New York Quarterly Foundation, Inc.
P. O. Box 2015
Old Chelsea Station
New York, NY 10113

www.nyqbooks.org

Copyright © 2011 by Mather Schneider

All rights reserved. No part of this book may be used or reproduced in any manner whatsoever without written permission of the author. This book is a work of fiction. Any references to historical events, real people or real locales are used fictitiously. Other names, characters, places, and incidents are products of the author's imagination, and any resemblance to actual events or locales or persons, living or dead, is entirely coincidental.

First Edition

Set in New Baskerville

Layout and Design by Raymond P. Hammond
Cover Drawing by Mather Schneider
Cover Layout and Design by Natalie Sousa

Library of Congress Control Number: 2011932515

ISBN: 978-1-935520-21-4

He Took a Cab

for Ara

Contents

HE TOOK A CAB / 15
WIFE / 16
THE PUSSY NEVER CAME DOWN / 17
I MISS YOU DIRK / 18
I'M SORRY I NEVER FIXED THE TOASTER / 20
HOBGOBLIN / 21
A COATIMUNDI ON A CRAPPY MONDAY / 22
TREASURE / 24
A BONE A DAY / 25
FEAST OR FAMINE / 26
THE LOST BARRIO / 27
THE MIDDLE OF JULY / 28
DARREN THE SHARK / 29
THE WHALE / 30
THE CRACK / 31
SERVICE / 32
A CABBY, NOT A CADDY / 33
THE VIRTUES OF SELF-LOCOMOTION / 34
AFTER A 14-HOUR SHIFT IN THE CAB / 36
DESTINY OF A CAB DRIVER / 37
SNOWBIRDS / 38
THE LAST COCA-COLA IN THE DESERT / 39
MY VERY GOOD FRIEND / 40
SUGAR AND WATER AND HEAT / 42
COCK BOY / 44
ACCEPTING THE NATURAL HIERARCHY / 45
MR. ENTHUSIASM / 46
AFTER TAKING A WRONG TURN / 47
SECRET SANTA / 48
THE THOUGHT THAT COUNTS / 49

THE LAW IN ORO VALLEY / 51
ZEN CABBY / 52
KISSING THE SNAKE / 53
SUZY Q RANCH / 54
PARKING / 55
CRUDDY BUDDIES / 56
FIVE BLOODY GRAND A WEEK / 57
MY FATHER IS AN ALIEN / 60
FILTHY PHIL / 61
ON THE WAY TO WHATABURGER / 62
WE ARE A SMOLDERING / 63
VIC'S BIG NOISE / 64
KITE WEATHER / 65
6234 N. KOLB AVE. / 67
THE HIGHLIGHT OF THE TUCSON STREET FAIR / 69
MOVING / 70
THE RED LAUGHING PHILOSOPHER… / 71
APOLOGIZE FOR NOTHING / 72
FREAK / 73
THE FIRST ANNIVERSARY OF OUR DIVORCE / 74
HOW DO YOU LIKE THEM APPLES? / 75
2 HOURS IS A LONG TIME / 76
SHANNON'S OASIS / 80
BLUE OX BLUES / 82
A MAN'S NEEDS / 83
SCOOTER / 84
TRUST ME / 85
SHITTY DRIVERS EVERYWHERE / 87
ANOREXIA NERVOSA / 88

1324 N. LANA HILLS DRIVE   / 89
PLEASE READ WITH YOUR CHILDREN...   / 91
DEVOTEE   / 93
SOMETIMES A CABBY   / 94
DROP TOWER   / 95
THE MEASLY SUBTRACTION   / 96
LORD OF THE WASPS   / 97
THREE LANES OF HELL   / 98
FLANK STEAK MY ASS   / 99
THE DRAG   / 101
THE ENVELOPE WITH THE BIG RED STAMP   / 102
STACY AND THE RENEGADE   / 104
WEDNESDAY NIGHT AT THE SURLY WENCH   / 105
THE MERGE   / 106
DOUBLETREE LIZ   / 107
MONSOON   / 108

In the old jazz argot, when it was said of someone, "He took a cab," that meant he died.

HE TOOK A CAB

A cabby got shot last night.
Another cabby found him.

He was already dead.
It was over where Geronimo

hits Main, between Larry's Hardware
and El Corral, thirty

feet from his cab. Our guess:
fare refused to pay

and fled; cabby pursued.
You know the hope

in your life is the same
as your hesitation,

before you stand up
to chase a man

down a dark alley,
for fourteen dollars.

WIFE

She told him she wanted to have a kid
and then she got the hiccups.

She tried holding her breath.
She tried sugar-water with a spoon in it.

She tried a cupful
of soda and bitters

while pinching her beer-porous nose
—like walking the plank—

nothing worked.
41 years old. That's when

she turned ugly. "Fuck
these fucking hiccups.

Somebody scare me, dammit! I need a man
to give me a good scare!

Doesn't anybody have any
balls around here?"

Like every other man in the bar
he just sat there

and waited for time
to cure them.

THE PUSSY NEVER CAME DOWN

To the bus station, please,
he says,
you got a girlfriend?

I met this girl last night,
he says,
you ever had a girl with a hare-lip?

He's forty some years old
with a face like a beehive.

She had a nice ass, he says,
and a wad of money
and she needed a drink
so we bought two bottles of Mad Dog
and went to the park
and after we drank those we went to The Mint
and that's when she went crazy.

Well we got kicked out of there and then
went back to her hotel where
some other broad was hanging out
and I thought shit
the pussy's coming down
but actually
the pussy never came down.

I tell you what, I was lucky
to get out of there with my life.

I got to get out of this town.
I'm going to San Diego.
I know this guy there has a used car lot
and he needs someone to stand out by the road
in a bear suit.

I MISS YOU DIRK

Dirk loved his blue cushion chair.
It was his only furniture.

He would have been
61 in June.

For 20 years he'd been outdoors
but he finally bumbled

into a state-paid apartment.
He was on the second floor

and in heaven.
To stay young, in the morning he sat in his chair

and lifted a big rock above his head.
Nights he sat there smoking

rollies and laughing
about his life and all

of life. He couldn't understand
why people wanted so much

and he never would,
but he was happy,

as happy as any cat
in the shade. He died there

like that, smiling in his chair
one summer night.

He was only 5 feet tall
and didn't leave much

of a dent
when they lifted him up

and took him away
to wherever it is

people like Dirk go.
The chair they just sat

out by the curb,
where he had found it.

I'M SORRY I NEVER FIXED THE TOASTER

You were beautiful even in the end
when you were so sick
of us.
Mornings I would sleep-walk in
and watch you
scraping away at the bitter rye
and knifing the yellow butter.
You would turn and smile
the way people smile
when they use too many front teeth
to bite into their blackened toast.
Then you'd tell me good morning
the way a woman does
when her mouth is full of ashes.

HOBGOBLIN

This young cabby drove his cab
into the cab yard at three in the morning.
He stopped crooked,
got out of his cab and gave a crazy look around
at the barbed wire fence,
the old tires,
the big cement plot of
lost bolts and oil stains.
He looked at the crummy cab office
like a mangy little cave
of a heart.
Then he peered into
the garage,
at a cab parked there
with its mouth open,
tonsils inflamed by a light bulb with a hook on it,
and just me and the mechanic
standing there,
a doctor and patient faced
with the truth.
His clothes were loose on his bones
and he'd grown a beard
and had the wet wild eyes
of an animal.
He dropped down
on his hands and knees
on the pavement,
let out a bloody,
beautiful howl
and then he ran off
into the night.

A COATIMUNDI ON A CRAPPY MONDAY

It's 5 a.m. and still dark
when I pull my cab up to trailer 82.
It's a medical voucher.
Information:
Ted Ols, 46, destination Kino Medical.
Ted slithers out of the trailer
and slits his eyes
in my headlights.
Did you see that? He hisses as he scurries
into the back of my cab.
What? I say. Where?
Over there, he says, something in the bushes...
I drive away slowly, crawling

over the speed-bumps.
This neighborhood's going to shit, he says.
The Mexican mob's takin' over.
Do you know what they're doing now? he says.
What? I say.
They're smuggling coatimundis, he says.
Coatawhats? I say.
Coatimundis, he says, from Mexico,
ugly hairy things, big
on the black market.
I found one under my trailer the other night, he says, I
heard a strange noise
and I got a broom and a flashlight
and I went outside and
looked underneath,
and these yellow fuckin' eyes
looked back at me.
I swear to god I could hear
the mother breathing.

In the dark he drills
holes in the back
of my head, and I try to make

myself as small
as possible.

TREASURE

She's got salt trails down her cheeks
and she's carrying a small plastic treasure chest
from an aquarium.
You can tell she used to drink a lot,
probably spent some time in jail
and on the streets,
forty-four years old.
"I'm Margie," she says,
getting into my taxi.
"Where to?" I say.
"The Valley Pet Clinic."
"What you got there?" I say.
"Oh, this is Chuy," she says.
"Chuy?" I say.
"He's a snail," she says.
"A snail for a pet?" I say.
"Chuy's a great pet," she says, "he comes
when I call him."
"I didn't even know snails had ears," I say.
"Here Chuy! Here Chuy!" she says.
She looks down and then
up at me in the rearview mirror.
"He's sick right now," she says.
"I'm sorry," I say.
"I bought him this to live in," she says, holding
the little treasure chest.
"His shell is the house God gave him
but everybody needs a little
extra protection,
right?"
"Right, Margie," I say.
And we both look out
our fish-bowl
at a world
that is just too big.

A BONE A DAY

If you're a cab driver
and you can make a hundred dollars per day
cash
that's pretty good.
If
at the end of a twelve-hour day
you've got a bone in your pocket
you're doing alright.
Nobody told you you'd get rich
but if you avoid head-ons
and side-swipes
and don't get mugged or held up
in traffic
then things might look your way
for a while.
Don't forget:
you always buy a lunch
and sometimes breakfast
and always a coffee
and cigarettes
and usually some gum or
a newspaper.
So if you've still got that bone
with you
at the end of the day,
be happy.

FEAST OR FAMINE

The turkey vulture digs out a dead snake's eyeball
and staggers on the yellow dotted line
like stitches
down the spine of the highway.
From the heat waves he looks at me—
bloody finger for a head—
as I bear down on him in my taxi.
I'm driving Mrs. Castilla and her grown daughter
to the doctor.
Mrs. Castilla has cancer
and her daughter keeps her company
when she goes to chemotherapy
three times a week.
Mrs. Castilla doesn't seem to be afraid of dying,
they are both usually as calm
as if they were just traipsing off
to the beauty parlor.
But at the sight of that snake
Mrs. Castilla starts screaming:
"OH GOD OH GOD OH MY GOD!"
Her daughter tells me her mom is terrified of snakes,
even dead ones.
She can hardly breathe through her choked sobs
and we are all on the verge
of panic,
all except for the vulture
who looks at us,
takes his prize and rises
into the clean blue air.

THE LOST BARRIO

One time long ago
when I first moved here to Tucson
and things were good
I drove around the city
and discovered a little barrio
with some artist shops and a cafe and
a slow quiet bar.
I spent the afternoon there
and for years I never went back.
I guess I didn't need to.
Then I got this job
driving cab
and my nerves are now raw from the 13-hour
nights
the coffee and cigarettes
and no exercise, the people coming at me
and any one of them could have
a gun or a knife,
and the intersections full of
suicides, and the lights blending
like supernovas...
While I was driving I figured I'd stumble upon that barrio
accidentally
and when I didn't I began
searching.
For weeks now I've been looking
and every day I put two hundred miles
on the gauge
and find nothing.
I've asked around.
The veteran taxi drivers shake
their heads no
and seem to be a bit sad and sorry
they can't help me
and it is the strangest
thing:
no one has any idea
what has happened.

THE MIDDLE OF JULY

It was hot as hell but otherwise
everything was fine at our little cab company
until Belinda
got hired.
Now arguments pop up everywhere
like backfire
and the gossip sticks
like spider web in your hair
and if you follow each strand
they all end
behind Belinda's red lips.
She started rumors:
Paul is a child molester,
Richard does coke off the front seat,
I have a dick like a cigarette. She has turned
our fares against us,
seduced our regulars,
laughed in our faces.
She cackles behind those two
canine incisors
and her fake boobs bounce and her
dyed blond hair hides
her pointed ears.
All her customers
think she's a saint
until one by one they
stop calling…
It's a hundred and ten
and rising.

We will meet Wednesday night
in the basement of the old church
to talk about our
future.

DARREN THE SHARK

He's a cab driver,
forty-five years old,
four feet ten inches tall
and all curled up
like a horseshoe.
It's easy to imagine a dorsal fin
on his little hunched back.
He's got fuzzy brown hair like a deranged peach
and a waist that starts right
below his man-tits,
and he's got short chubby arms
like an alligator.
His ex-old lady was five eleven and
three hundred pounds
but she ran off with a trucker
with a cyst on his neck
like a red buoy.
Darren kind of sneaks up on you
in the office when us cab drivers are paying
our leases
and out in the field
he'll shark a fare from you quicker
than you can take a leak.
He can barely see through glasses thick
as fingernails
and he's nearly deaf
but that look in his cold eye is enough
for you to steer clear.
He navigates by instinct—
smelling the blood
after bar rush,
driving the drunks home, pocketing
their sloppy money.
His secret is
he never sits still,
always moving, always moving—
that or die.

THE WHALE

He's fifty-five years of smug blubber,
a bored heir of a lucky fortune
who can barely walk on the vestiges of his legs
floating in the lobby of the fancy hotel
like a giant aquarium.
He's waiting for another cabby,
a Town Car or something, but I shark him
and drive him to the casino
where he blows
thirty grand a month.
It's hard to understand fear or humility
when you know you can eat
everything in your path.
His mate mooncows beside him
like a somnolent mirror image
on this sunny afternoon,
rays filtering down through the thick blue sky
into the windows of my cab
where the dust rises
like plankton.
His voice is a screechy violin
and I'm just another suckerfish
in his armpit.
It's like I'm in an undersea vessel
that's gone too deep:
my ears plug up;
the crack in my windshield
jumps one inch
at a time.

THE CRACK

There is a crack
in my taxi's
windshield

like something
coming
unfrozen.

I stare
around it
while driving
back to town

after dropping
an old man
at the airport.

It's a beautiful
day
except
for that crack.

The sun
runs a tongue
on the edge
of my face.

SERVICE

A purple El Dorado nearly runs
me off the road
then gives me the horn and the
finger.
Fuck you, I whisper.
I'm driving my taxi
and there's an old woman in my back seat.
I'm taking her to church
on St. Patrick's Day morning.
She will sit in the front pew
and she will sing "Danny Boy"
at the end of the service.
I will sit in the parking lot of the church
in my taxi
and listen to her sing
out the open church doors
in the morning sun.
It's the most important thing
in the world:
I'm driving a little old woman
in a green hat
to Our Mother of Sorrows,
and I've got to get her there safe.

A CABBY, NOT A CADDY

I saw a cougar on the road
near the five-star golf course hotel
in the desert outside of town.
I was in my cab, going the other way.
I had just dropped off a fat business man
with his heavy bag of golf clubs
like a body bag with a skeleton
rattling and knocking around.
I'd fumbled with the bag and had trouble
balancing it on the flagstone
(as the hotel bellhops snickered)
and then the stiff
didn't even tip me.
I'm a cabby, not a caddy.
It was the middle of the morning
and already hot
and I had made forty-five dollars
when I saw it: two or three seconds at most
loping across the sunny pavement
golden fur thick and clean
muscles moving like heat-waves
strong tongue licking blood
from white muzzle.
It fed off the small game attracted
to the golf course,
this giant blob of emerald mercury
pulsing in the sand.
The arid hills stretched out behind me
as I drove back down to town,
where insane dogs are kept
in cages
and pigeons
make par everywhere.

THE VIRTUES OF SELF-LOCOMOTION

The superiority of school bus drivers
grates on my nerves,
these wiry-haired moralists
immune from street law,
sitting so high and mighty,
running red lights and careening around corners
like great leaning walls
of tiger-striped death.
When I was a kid the bus drivers
were always mentally ill
and more interested in spanking our bottoms
than getting us home.
They kept their perverted eyeballs
in the overhead mirror
instead of on the road
and they'd leave you if you weren't
standing out there
in the rain or snow
like a good boy.
Now it's thirty years later
and I'm driving a cab
and I'm still being cock-blocked
by those smug mothers
hissing their diesel like the sooty halitosis
of a fifty-year-old smoker
tongue-kissing a sixth grader.
Like puss-filled centipedes
the size of railroad cars
they barrel yellow and mad through the city
cutting people off
endangering every life
along their sacred route

but when they come to
a screeching stop
to puke out their defiled darlings
they swing their little flipper
stop sign out the side
and good god all the world better
just freeze.

AFTER A 14-HOUR SHIFT IN THE CAB

The fan hums at
5:31 p.m.

and the humans are
tired.

The birds
are cheered out

and the flies
fall like hollow

raisins.
A coffee makes

my forehead sweat
and an ice cube

hisses
in a cup of tears.

Society is
not life.

DESTINY OF A CAB DRIVER

Until someone needs me
I have no reason to be.
I have no destination of my own.
I spend my life driving in circles
and never get any closer
to the center.
I meet a lot of people in my cab
and it's true:
no man has the answers
for another.
My life intersects
with theirs,
I learn a little of their own circles
which also will not seem to break
and if I'm lucky
I feel a tickle
of familiar struggle.
But when they get to where
they want to go
I can't follow.
I'm again left floating alone
in a purposeless void,
chained to my cab
like karma.

SNOWBIRDS

The brightly plumed couple totters off
American flight two twenty-two from Chicago.
They stretch their wings in the warm Arizona air
then climb into my cab
and I take them to their million dollar winter home
in the foothills.
They're about sixty.
She's never worked, he retired early
from the family business.
They both sport golf course tans
and whitened teeth.
The woman has eye-watering breath
like she's been eating raw lizards,
the man is a pillow-faced imbecile
with white feathers and hollow bones.
"I was thinking of tea and sandwiches
on Thursday," the woman says.
"Sounds good," the man says.
"Maybe a guitarist," she says.
"Not that last guy," he says.
"Heavens, no."
The pioneers tamed the desert
for people like this.
The Indians were murdered
for people like this.
I drop them at their golden nest.
A tiny brass coyote sits on their mailbox,
its head thrown to the cast
iron sun.

THE LAST COCA-COLA IN THE DESERT

Jose knows he's the last
Coca-Cola in the desert.
He's two hundred thirty pounds packed
onto a five seven frame,
forty-two years old,
has rotten teeth
and a habitually stuffed up
and runny nose.
You can't understand his English
or his Spanish.
He's a waiter at El Fuego.
I drive him to work in my cab
and he always tells me of his girlfriends
here and abroad
and how good he's got it
and how great life is.
He's got acne
and no money
and he breathes with his mouth open
and his wrinkled shirt sticks
out of his dirty pants
and his dove white socks
fall on his coal black shoes.
Every girl we pass on the street
he whispers about
and pokes me in the shoulder
if I don't laugh.
He lives alone, hasn't had
sex without paying for it
in five years,
doesn't have a car
and barely holds his job.
His feet stink
but he's unstoppable.
He's the last Coca-Cola in the desert
and he knows it.

MY VERY GOOD FRIEND

He had a red plastic cup of something
in one hand and
a half sandwich in the other
and he came running up to my cab
while I was stopped at the red light.

Shit, I said, get in.

He climbed in and spilled some of his drink
on the gray vinyl.
He looked like he was from India.

My friend, he said, good day to you.

He was slightly out of breath.

How ya doing? I said.

Can you please to take me to university? he said.

Sure, I said.

I only have one problem, he said.

What's that?

I don't have any money, he said.

Get out.

Wait, he said, I have
a little money.

How much?

I have 10 dollars.

It's 25 to the university.

Wait, he said, I think I
might have 15 dollars.

25 to the university, I said
and pulled over on a side street to
let him out.

Tell you what, he said,
because I am tired and
because I am already here, I will
pay you 17 dollars.

Get out.

He got out and stood there.

Ok, he said through the window,
for you my friend
I think I have 20 dollars.

Jesus Christ, I said,
let's go.

He got in again.

I'm gonna need that 20 now.

Of course my friend,
he said,
my very good friend,
of course,
I have it right here.

Can you break a hundred?

SUGAR AND WATER AND HEAT

We put up a hummingbird feeder
and they come almost immediately.
This amazes my Mexican girlfriend—
how easy it is:
just sugar and water and heat.
She's thirty-four years old
and never would've believed it.
She was born in Hermosillo
and her life has been spent working
with her head down.
This is what she has been taught
she is for:
to be taken advantage of.
The feeder hangs out the back sliding glass door
and we watch the hummers come
in the morning
and in the late afternoons.
She calls a Mexican girlfriend of hers
who lives in California
and tells her about the hummingbird feeder.
This girl is just like her:
her life is nothing but work,
3 jobs,
seven days a week.

"You just put the feeder out there,
my girlfriend tells her,
and they come and eat it
like it's a flower,
they poke their long thin beaks in
and hover so easy
and beautiful
and their wings sound like a big bee
but you're not afraid."

When she hangs up the phone
she comes to me.
My amiga is jealous,
she says.
They don't have hummingbirds
in California.

COCK BOY

The Food City grocery building
is massive and solid
in the fat-boiling summer afternoons
around here.
Sometimes I'll park my cab
in its shade.
It's nice to have a few moments
to myself
just breathing
and daydreaming
out of the heat of the sun.
On the side of the building
someone has spray painted
"COCK BOY"
in parrot blue
two-foot-tall lettering
about head high.
Sometimes I think
the writer was interrupted
and the thought
was left unfinished.
Other times I am certain
it's complete
and whole
as it is.

ACCEPTING THE NATURAL HIERARCHY

The brown-toothed mouth-breather in the
roid-rage truck
rocks and rolls on my
bumper for a block,
cusses and guns it and then
grabs his chance and roars by me
like I'm going backwards,
jerks in front of me
with the whip of his stink-eye
before stomping his brake
at a red light smack
in his big fat face.
I come to a stop
behind him
and sit, calmly, calmly, so very
humbled
as
a driver
and
as a man.

MR. ENTHUSIASM

He leans against his cab
in the cab queue at the Holiday Inn.
He's hunched over,
has balding hair
and puts both hands in his
big loose pockets.
Every time he exhales he sighs.
He has wide hips
and sloped shoulders
and a low-slung flabby belly
like a half-full feed bag.
I pull in behind him.
"How long you been
waiting?" I ask
while getting out of my cab.
"Oh," says Mr. Enthusiasm,
"Maybe a half hour.
Maybe an hour."
Just then five Asian girls walk toward us.
"We need taxi," one
of them says,
but they can't all fit in
Mr. Enthusiasm's car.
My taxi is a van
and so we all pile in.
I look at Mr. Enthusiasm
as I drive away.
"Sorry," I say.
He shrugs.
Earlier I'd rubbed Radi's shoulder
at the Greyhound bus station.
Radi is a cab driver too.
He's a Buddhist from India
and is always full of good cheer.
If you rub him you'll have good luck
    all day.

AFTER TAKING A WRONG TURN

I'm a cab driver, which means I deal
with traffic.
To avoid traffic
is to avoid the herd: impossible.
But to try to avoid it
is the ultimate challenge.
Whatever the herd would do,
do the opposite, but I can't just go
in the opposite direction all
the time, I'd wind up
in Yuma or somewhere, lost, no, I need to get
to where I need to get to,
I need money, I need fares,
I need to go about
the same old thing, only differently. I'm a city
person, I know how
the herd thinks,
and stinks,
but sometimes there are simply no
alternative routes outside
of driving across
the courthouse lawn.
I'm in a trap and I can't get out
of my own way—
the stoplight does
its macabre swing
and I end up idling on Main Street and Congress
with the rest of the honking
fuming dipshits, pinned to our hot seats
like death moths,
like pigs jammed onto the spit
screaming and tubercular, coughing the
stars to shreds.
The smell of exhaust like death
follows me
all the way
home.

SECRET SANTA

At the cab company my boss coerced us
into drawing names out of a bag
at Christmas time.
The idea was to buy a 10 dollar gift
for whoever's name you drew
and exchange them
at an employee party at
the Pack 'Em Inn.
This is despite the fact that hardly any of us
get along
and some of us even hate each other and have
nearly come to blows.

Well I drew Dan's name
and bought him a 10 dollar gift certificate
for gasoline at the C&T
and Dan drew Nancy and got her
2 cans of Budweiser and
a box of Snow Balls
and Gene got Roger
a pizza and
Roger got Paul a hat a
monkey wouldn't wear.

Nobody seemed to have a gift for me
which pissed me off
until I learned later
that while he was driving to the Christmas party
Robert was pulled over
and arrested
for possession of a 10 dollar bag
of blow
with my name on it.

THE THOUGHT THAT COUNTS

Me and Josie got in a fight last night
so this morning I drive my taxi over to Mister Donut
and buy a box of donut holes
for her.
She really loves donut holes,
so do I,
who doesn't,
but before I can deliver them to her
I get a fare from dispatch.
When I arrive at the static-filled address
I find a forgotten hotel
and four dark Saudi dudes standing around smoking
and looking at their watches.
They are dressed in black Western suits and have a square
ton of luggage
which they watch me put in the trunk.
Then they all pile in.
"It's twenty five bucks to the airport," I say.
They bitch and grumble,
but agree.
When we see the sign for Delta Airlines
they argue amongst each other
about who is to pay
until finally one of them reluctantly hands me
some shiny bills,
like he's handing over his firstborn child
or the keys to his Mercedes
and then he demands exact change
and a blank receipt.
I throw their luggage on the pavement
and drive off.
Then immediately I get another dispatch call
and I have to go even further
away from Josie,

wondering if I'll ever get the chance
to make things right.
But a half-mile down the road I realize
it doesn't matter anyway,
because the Saudis stole my donut holes.

THE LAW IN ORO VALLEY

In my taxi I drive a rich white woman
from Oro Valley
to her company Fourth of July party.
She is a recent U of A graduate
from wealthy parents.
She's maybe twenty-eight
and nowhere near
as good looking as
she thinks.
She's accompanied by an overgrown frat boy
who is reading the newspaper
(on the way to the
Fourth of July party, yes)
and he says,
"Fifty-four people have died
in the last month
trying to cross the border
into Arizona."
Mexico is forty-five minutes from here.
In fact the woman I love
and live with is Mexican.
The other woman looks out the cab window
and says,
"Well, I'm glad they died."
The man looks at her with something
that is almost horror,
almost human.
"They're breaking the law,"
she says,
"they deserve it."
The man says nothing.
At the stop sign I stop
a little too long
until the guy in the black truck behind me
slams his fist into his
horn,
and holds it there.

ZEN CABBY

All the lights turn green at your approach
and there's a warm breeze
and your haircut grew in good
and your jeans are clean and loose.
Cab driving is like gambling:
it needs abandon to be done well.
Cars swerve out of your way
in the nick of time
and each call from dispatch
is exactly where you are
and you see each fare
before they see you.
You can't be afraid
to lose.
You barely miss the train
and the cop
and the funeral procession
and you always have exactly the change you need
and when one fare cancels
another calls.
Some call you lucky
and cuss you
when they see you sitting in your cab
in the hot slow afternoon
in the shade
not worrying about money.
The trick is to trust nothing
but the deepest laws,
and the only way to trust
is to let go.

KISSING THE SNAKE

The microphone of my cab's two-way radio
has a long curly tail
and big black head.
There are certain rules about handling it:
don't interrupt people,
press the button,
count to three before you talk,
watch for the red light
and release the button afterwards.
Some cabbies use the radio like a morphine drip:
they can't stomach the outer space pull
and the purposelessness.
They can't breathe alone.
There's a lot of down-time
out here.
The radio is not a toy,
it's a talisman,
a tool,
a work-aide
the fastest life-line during trouble, and trouble
is inevitable.
The radio is like a mirror to the heart.
Some yell into the radio,
some whisper,
some whine,
some laugh,
some snivel and bawl.
Some people feel naked behind the radio
and some feel incredibly brave.
You have to remember the voice
on the other end
is a human being
and the most important thing of all to learn
is how to just sit
and listen.

SUZY Q RANCH

This guy climbs into my cab at the airport
and he wants to go to the nudist retreat
out in the desert.
It's about twenty minutes away.
On the drive out
I think about that poor guy I saw
last year.
It was a Saturday night at Upper Crust
and I was having a slice of pizza
when this completely naked guy ran in.
He tried to order a calzone
like he really needed
it badly,
but the service wasn't fast enough
and a bunch of cops ran in
and jumped him and dragged
him outside.
Three cops got the naked guy
face down on the concrete sidewalk,
knees in his back,
while people of Saturday night
looked on,
well dressed people gasping and gawking
and laughing
the ugliest of laughs
and the cops leaned into him harder as he
squirmed and cried.
I felt bad for him.
This nudist retreat out in the desert
has a Wild West theme
with bungalows and a fake saloon with
swinging doors,
like a ghost town haunted
by naked people.
It costs two hundred dollars a day,
but that includes
everything.

PARKING

Love is a heart drawn
on a steamed up window.

Wipe it away:
a cop's face staring in.

CRUDDY BUDDIES

Don and Kathy are both on parole
and there's not much else they can do
except hack,
so they share a taxi: he drives nights
and she drives days.
They both live at the Parker Suites
on Prince Street
with its pool of fungus
and biweekly gunfire.
Kathy used to work at McDonald's
but stole 10 grand from the safe
and got ratted out
and nabbed over by Yin Yang's Liquor.
Don is an old jack-o-lantern
caving in,
an avowed-since-Friday catholic
barely one step ahead
of a meth habit.
If it's not love,
it works for now.
He gives her a ride
to her community service job
and she gives him a ride
to his urinalysis.

FIVE BLOODY GRAND A WEEK

There's an expensive detox clinic up in the foothills
called Cottonwood de Tucson.
It's built in a cottonwood grove.
I drive a British woman up there
in my taxi.

I've come from England to meet a friend of mine
she says.

You're a good friend
I say.

Very good
she says.

Did you know that place
costs five bloody grand a week?
she says.

Holy moly
I say.

It's a long drive to Cottonwood
through the desert.

Have you been to the Grand Canyon?
she says.

I'm embarrassed to
say no
I say.

I figured if I was gonna come all this way
I should see the Grand Canyon.

Understandable.

I cried when I saw it
she says.
I cry all the time.

You'll feel right at home at Cottonwood.
I say.

The counselors are worried
my friend hasn't cried yet.

If he's paying five grand a week
I say
he'd better cry.

British men don't cry
she says.

Very good, then.

It should be easy not to drink
she says.

You would think so.

Just don't drink
she says.

Right.

I don't drink
she says.

I don't
say anything.

When I drop her off the sun
is going down.
The cottonwood trees are shedding
like crematory ash
as I tool out of there
thinking I really should go
and see
the Grand Canyon.

MY FATHER IS AN ALIEN

who blends into the crowd
as he waits at the airport.

I'm thirty-eight
and he asks me if I've grown.

The gray in my hair
is like his last

I saw him. At least time
has kept its word.

We hug like squeezing by someone
in an airplane aisle,

arms turnstiles,
bodies hard as suitcases,

before working our way
to the big round lip

of the baggage claim.
I still have his elbows,

hands and shoulders.
In five minutes we are silent.

Eyes thirst for their own
among the bags that descend

no two exactly alike, all falling
into the same slow orbit.

FILTHY PHIL

He's fifty-eight years old
and has three daughters,
Eve, Serenity and Pleasant,
but he hasn't seen them in a while.
He was held hostage in Vietnam,
became a hippy when he got home,
spent time in prison for computer fraud,
started a meth lab after that
and finally gave that up and now is
driving a cab.
He's got this wrinkly face
and eternal toothless smile
like a tall old
baby, kind
of,
as he shoves his cigs at you
and talks and bullshits for hours
leaning on his cab.
His latest plan is to marry a Russian girl
whose family will pay him
fifteen grand a year
for five years,
then he'll be
free and clear.
Hopefully you can use
your own judgment:
he's no good at love
but neither
is anyone else.
Just don't loan him anything
or let him breathe
on you.

ON THE WAY TO WHATABURGER

Girard is a 415 pound spiritualist.
He's 31
and has never worked a day in his life.
His mother pays for everything.
He has a Mercedes but he won't drive it
so I drive him around town in my cab.

One day on the way to Whataburger
me and Girard saw two cars
collide head-on.
We had a close view of one of the drivers
jerked hard and held by his seat belt
like a crash test dummy.

In the following days Girard had chronic pain
exactly where a seat belt would be.
He called it a "sympathetic injury".
I took him to the mall
and to his new age bookstore
and to the movies
and to his shrink
and he complained about this ailment
to a clairvoyant
who said it proved he was a sensitive
and superior person
in touch with the agony of the
universe.

One day he telephoned me
in tears.
I drove him to the emergency room
where they found an intestinal blockage
right where a seat belt would be.

And they didn't seem very sympathetic
about it.

WE ARE A SMOLDERING

of the oldest symbol
and every morning we get up
and do it again
and the sad and beaten sit in church on Sundays
like cats crying
at the doors of strangers.
Some people live too long
and others die on the cross
and morality is the last hieroglyph
on the last hill.
I want to be aroused
in the hour of no cities,
placental flame lapping the wound
of knowledge,
eyes in the sliced shadows
staring into it
like animals
on the precipice of insight,
a new hot wind
in my face.

VIC'S BIG NOISE

Vic was eighty-four years old
and still drove a cab.
He had white hair growing out of his ears
like albino rhubarb.
Toward the end Vic was getting loopy.
He bought himself a small plastic battery-powered
fart machine
at the Dollar Tree
and it became the center of his existence.
He drove his beat up old cab around
and shot the shit with the other cabbies.
He'd activate his fart machine for us
and laugh like hell every time.
It sounded just like
a real fart.
Old Vic, he was a hoot.
He finally made his big noise
the day he crashed his cab
into the plate glass
of Al's Barber.

KITE WEATHER

I drive Miss Carr to her kidney dialysis
in my taxi at 5 a.m.

She's 43 and clutches
a ratty blanket.

At the clinic she lays back
on a gray vinyl bed-chair

with several other liver-lidded pilgrims
who look like they've been raped

three days a week for years and years.
The machine reaches in

to her with its deep breathy hum
and the cruel tubes slurp

out her blood and pump
it back in purple, sterile

and cold. Five hours later
she is released

and I take her home. Stopped
at a red light I see a city park

kitty-corner. A boy holds a string
leading to a yellow kite

a mile up in the blue sky.
Look at that, I say.

Miss Carr smiles and
lifts her head from her chest

like an anchor.
Her mouth is a taut line

slackening for a moment,
a flash in the sun, and then the light

changes and we move on,
everything

getting smaller and
smaller

behind
us.

6234 N. KOLB AVE.

It was dumb luck I got
the call at all
and then I couldn't find the address
until I saw a man standing out
in the sunny road
waving his arms at my cab.

He had a brown dog in a carrier
and he put that in the back seat of my cab and
then he got in front.
I took him to the airport
which was almost an hour ride.
He told me he was going on his
first vacation in 22 years.
On the way we talked about
politics and film and academics
and health care and
children and wives, sports, we covered
it all, getting
nowhere, agreeing with each other,
laughing.

When I pulled into the airport his
phone rang
and someone on the other side
told him his father just had a
heart attack.
His father lived on
the other side of town.
He sat there next to me in the cab
at DEPARTURES.
"Turn around" he said,
"Take me to the hospital."

It was a much quieter ride to the hospital.
At one point his phone rang again.
He listened for a few seconds
and then hung up.
"He's dead," he said to me,
"You can slow down."

At the hospital it came
to 120 bucks.
He paid without a sound and
even tipped me.
Then he walked away.
"Hey," I said, "What about
your dog?"
"Shit," he said,
turned around and came back to the
cab.
He hauled the thumping dog cage out
and set it on the hot
concrete driveway.
"Sorry Sammy," he said.

I smiled at him and drove slowly
away,
wondering where
the next call would
come from.
You could make an educated guess
and experience helped
but in the end you
just never
knew.

THE HIGHLIGHT OF THE TUCSON STREET FAIR

The mouse sits
on top of the cat

and the cat sits
on top of the dog

and the dog walks
tongue hanging out

and the long leash
dips down and up

to a wiry six foot
six inch rocker chick.

MOVING

Gangrene light of the city
11 o'clock on Wednesday night
a woman talks to the cab driver
while her daughter who is about five
sits looking out at the city.
When are we moving, mommy?

The mother turns her head
to reveal a gourd-like face.

Moving? mom says.
Waddya mean moving?
We're not moving.
You think we're moving?
The damn kid thinks we're moving.

Ok, mom says,
the other night we *talked* about moving
maybe in a *while*
like maybe in *February*
BUT NOT NOW! My god,
moving?

I told her we're not moving,
I *told* you we're not moving.
I mean if we were going to move
I sure wouldn't mind
but who's got money to move?
Not me! Not us!
Anyway we're not moving
so I wish you'd quit asking me,
I wish she'd quit asking me.
Moving ha!

The child looks out the window
like an amused Buddha.
The cab driver is silent as the Thames.

THE RED LAUGHING PHILOSOPHER OF THE TAR PAPER SHACK

Beans are boiling,
sex and salt,
fire and spit,
and I'm alone but not
hungry for long,
what's there to lament,
so many histories dead
like the people who taught us
what love is: it is both
butter and steel,
tomatoes and garlic
on the teeth of a shark
in the churning cartilage
of a dream,
beans are boiling like brown labs
fighting over a dead duck
in the muck of a pond mother nature is reclaiming
      in a murmur,
           in a millennium,
beans spilling over in unrest telling me to
taste the sunset,
laugh first and last,
bide dark riders of iron diligence,
beware the hunger of the last coyote
on the last ridge
    of the moon,
        chasing a shadow animal with no gravity
          over a hill of dust.

APOLOGIZE FOR NOTHING

I know you think I think
you're a geek, but I wouldn't want you
any other way. You can't trust
the trendy, the slick,
the hipper-than-thou, you can't
barter with the well-adjusted.
In fact there's something sexy
about your soft drink bottle
glasses, your androgynous coverings,
the way your mousy hand
scurries to your mouth when you laugh,
your short hair thin and straight
as if it lay all night pressed
between the pages of the Iliad.
There is an epic written
on your naked neck, white as the inside of a shell,
which you attribute to the only good
gene your sister didn't confiscate.
At the bar it's adorable
the way you verbally doggy paddle,
a city girl in the country lake
of drunken babble, hesitating, rethinking everything,
opening and closing
your tab three times. It's ok,
I too am embarrassed to be alive.
Talk to me in the beautiful
but singularly uncheerleader-like octaves of your voice,
and I will ease myself down
from the barn roof of loneliness.
Apologize for nothing one more time
and I swear I'll kiss you.

FREAK

The call girl comes in and looks down
at all my shoes, which I keep by the door.
It seems a natural place to keep them.
"Why do you keep all your shoes by the door?" she asks.
"I don't know," I say. "Where do you keep yours?"
"Well," she says, "I keep one pair by the door
sometimes, but the rest I keep in the closet."
"My closet's full," I say.
"Where is the closet?" she says.
"There," I say.
"I mean," she says, "it's like you've got a whole
Oriental thing going here or something, all
these shoes by the door."
"I have always kept them there," I say.
"Really?" she says, "It just seems strange."
Finally she comes over
to the bed.
Afterwards, while dressing, she looks
again at my shoes and shakes
her head and laughs.
When she's gone, I sit staring at those shoes by the door,
feeling like some kind of freak.

THE FIRST ANNIVERSARY OF OUR DIVORCE

The air is brisk
and the dew undisturbed
on the lifeguard's footholds.

It's early,
only a few people are in the pool.
When it gets crowded

someone will insist on sharing a lane
and then I'll have to meet him
or her

each length going
and coming,
our arms flying while trying so hard

not to slap each other,
waiting on the moment
when we both bring our heads up

and lunge for the same air.
But right now I have my own.
I slip into the prenatal gravity

and plunge face-under.
The pressure massages my vodka head
as I begin my walrus crawl

across the lilting surface. 36
laps make a half mile.
I like this place—

it isn't considered strange
to be quiet;
or to have red eyes.

HOW DO YOU LIKE THEM APPLES?

I had to pick a lady up
at an old farts home
so I arrived early
and parked my cab out
front and went up the ramp
and into the
lobby.
It was very quiet and clean
and there was an old
lady behind the desk.
I told her I had come
to pick up a Mrs. Hefrin.
She phoned a room.
She'll be right
down, the lady told me.

I stood there getting hot flashes
and twiddling my thumbs.

Here she is,
the old lady behind the desk
said as another lady,
not quite so old,
came walking down the hall.

Mrs. Hefrin? I said.

That's me, she said, thanks for coming,
I was visiting my
aunt but it's time
to go home.

On the way to the door we passed
a bowl of apples on the counter
which had been set there for
people to take.

Can I have an apple? I said.

No, no, the lady
behind the desk said,
those are for guests and
residents,
they're not for
cab drivers and people
like that.

Oh, I said, withdrawing
my hand.
Me and Mrs. Hefrin gave each other
a look.

Then Mrs. Hefrin said,
Can I have an apple?

Well of COURSE, the lady
behind the desk said.

Thank you, Mrs. Hefrin said, and
took one.

Then Mrs. Hefrin and I left,
me carrying her luggage and her
carrying the apple.

How about that? I said in the cab.
Mrs. Hefrin handed me the
apple.
Are you sure? I said, these are
like gold around here.
She laughed.

People get strange when they get
old, she said, Lord knows
I'm getting strange
myself, it's
hard.

I guess it
is, I said.

After I dropped her
at the airport
I took a bite of the apple
and gagged.
It was the mushiest piece of
shit apple that ever
rolled down
God's weedy
highway.

TWO HOURS IS A LONG TIME

He gets in my cab after stumbling
out of the Buffet Tavern.
Third and Eighth, he says
and looks out the window.
Halfway there he starts talking:
You want to hear something, man?
Sure, I say.
Last year I was in my truck
and I thought I could make it
across the Santa Cruz River,
you know,
it had been raining heavy
but I thought I could make it.
Let's just say I didn't make it…
I was dead when they dragged me out.
They put me in a body bag
and took me to the morgue.
An hour later as they were opening the bag
I just came back to life.
No one has been able to understand it,
the doctors are mystified.
But, here I am.

Later I told my wife I didn't see
any lights or tunnels and there weren't any
voices or god damned spirit guides.
There was blackness
and nothingness
a dark silence
that went on and on.
Well, she went to stay with her mother
in Yuma.
I don't blame her.
two hours is a long time.

I'm not a brave man, you know?
But, I slept in Death's bed
and I learned Death's secrets.

I learned it has no secrets.

SHANNON'S OASIS

Shannon was born four months premature
to a crackhead mom.

She was so small
you could see her heart

like a goldfish
under paper-thin ice.

The hospital lights ripped and ruined
her tiny retinas

and the doctors didn't give her
a month

but somehow here she is
30 years later

blindly limping toward my taxi on
taffy legs

with Lloyd,
her loyal yellow lab

guiding the way.
Lloyd climbs into the cab,

sinks to the floor
with a happy huff

and then Shannon feels her way
like a spelunker.

When she's comfortable
I drive her to the public pool

where she will sit, so peaceful,
under her dark umbrella,

moving her hand in
and out of the shade.

BLUE OX BLUES

There's a thirty-foot-tall statue of Paul Bunyon
who my Mexican girlfriend calls
Bob Onion.
He stands on the corner of Stone and Glenn
which I pass in the hot afternoon
on my way home from driving my cab all day.
He hulks there with his big square jaw
smiling in the power lines.
He wears a well-trimmed black French Canadian beard
and a good-natured woodchopper's shirt
faded red like a dying lily
with the sleeves rolled up to reveal
log-jam forearms and giant easy-boy hands
gripping a grand-daddy
of an ax.
His legs are like blue-denim Stonehenge
and his boots are as big
as black baby strollers.
He stares down into the traffic
and he appears to lean forward
like he might just fall face
first into the intersection.
What he's doing here in Tucson
standing on the tumbleweed corner
holding in a sneeze
is a mystery...
Maybe he thinks he needs a tan.
Maybe he's looking for his blue ox Babe.
Whatever the reason,
when I see him I know
I'm almost home.

A MAN'S NEEDS

Four call girls, two black, two white
have come from Phoenix
to work Tucson
for the weekend.
I pick them up
in my cab
from the Greyhound bus station
and take them to a hotel.
The whole time they're taking
phone calls:
"Issuh hunret fowa
half ouwa
and two hunret
fowa ouwa."
They look at me
like snakes with chipped
diamonds for eyes
and reply to my "Nice day, huh?"
with the thick silence
of cold blood.
I want to leave
their overpriced cunts
at the first corner
but the truth is I am not
so different from them
and so I eat
my pride and drive.
At the hotel I palm
their money
and put it in my pants
even knowing
where it's been.

SCOOTER

She's thirty-six and ugly as a gargoyle
and here she is in my cab
with her Tom Selleck mustache
her wine barrel body
her arthritis and depression and migraines and backaches
her peroxide blond hair frizzy
as death by chair
her bound-sausage feet and Michelin Man legs
her two-ham ass
her blood-blossoms of acne
mixed with cheap makeup
like strawberry icing on her foul cake face.
She rolls the window up
to within an inch
and lights a smoke.
She hasn't had a job in fifteen years
lets other people take care of her
like this free ride home from the doctor
because she hurt her foot
walking to the bathroom
high as a kite on her prescription narcotics.
All the way to her government-subsidized house she bitches
because nobody will give her
a free scooter.
And when I get close to her house
I miss her street accidently
(I've never been there before)
and I have to stop and turn around
and she snickers and snorts
like I'm the biggest
fool ever
to limp
across the piss-poor earth.

TRUST ME

The man and woman had been partying all night
and they had a greasy smugness
on their young faces. It was 7 a.m.
and they reeked
of smoke and sex and tequila
as they climbed into my cab outside
the Riverpark Inn.
He barked a drunken address at me and we
dropped the woman off first
over by Craycroft and Seneca.
He kissed her foul
mouth for a full minute and watched her
wobble away.
Then he told me where he lived.
Over by the jail? I said.
Yup, he said, I work there,
I'm a guard.
He flashed his ID badge
and sneered.
Ever been there? he said.
I knew what he meant.
No, I lied.
You don't want to get mixed
up with that scum, he
said, I work with those losers every day,
I've seen it all,
trust me.
He wanted me to stop
a block from his house
so his wife wouldn't
see the taxi.
Drop dead,
I thought
as he walked away
across his neighbor's lawn

but he didn't
fall,
he staggered but he
didn't fall.

SHITTY DRIVERS EVERYWHERE

Each day murder bolts through my heart a hundred times,
I toss "bitch" and "asshole"
around like confetti.
Maybe they're on their cell phone
or maybe they're too bunny-footed
to turn right on red
or maybe they just have a dumb
look on their face.
Mainly I'm mad because I'm forced
to go among them
and compete with them
and it seems like many of them enjoy it
and would not change it
even if they could.
Maybe that's why I stick knives
into people and blow heads off with
shotguns and chuck car bombs through
windows a dozen times a day,
roaring my private fire
like a dragon in a mini van.
I don't know anything personal
about those I'm dismissing
as stupid and subhuman,
and maybe that's the secret
to banishing them all to hell.

ANOREXIA NERVOSA

You shiver at the thought
of being touched,

understand too well
what hunger wants,

are only home
in the emptiness
that follows purging,

terrified of what
brought you here

like a skeleton loping
through the ashes
of an old pueblo.

I miss how you used to reach
around me
take my cigarette
for a drag
and place it
back in my fingers.

It was as if you needed me
and maybe you did.

Now I know that need
is qualified

and sadness
can live
on almost nothing.

1324 N. LANA HILLS DRIVE

Sorry if I stink, he said,
I wear a colostomy bag
and they gave me the wrong liners
last time.

I don't smell anything, I lied, as I pulled
my cab out of the wide
smooth driveway
twisting away from the huge millionaire's house
on the little hill on the
west side of town.

It's my mother's house, he said,
I'm living with her because
I'm dying.

He was around 45.

She's a bitch, he said, rich people
are all fucked up.
I just want a small room
with a computer
and enough money for food.
I want to start eating good,
he said.

I took him to the store
where he got a gallon of milk
and colostomy liners.

He chugged the milk on the way home
leaving white foam around his mouth.

When I stopped the cab inside
the pearly gates
he thanked me, paid, got out and
went back in the house.

It's a huge, beautiful house. I had
always wondered who lived there.

PLEASE READ WITH YOUR CHILD FIFTEEN MINUTES A DAY

is written on the billboard
by the Whataburger
at Benson and Freemont.
The lady in the back of my cab says,
"Shit,
I used to read to my kid all the time
but the little slut ended
up getting pregnant when she was
14 and running off with the guy. Then
after she had a miscarriage she
came home, got fucking
pregnant again with another guy,
but she was hooked on crack that
time and the baby came
out dead.
That really messed
her up,
but it didn't stop her sucking
on that pipe,
fuck no.
Eventually she got clean and
got pregnant again even though
the doctors told her not to
(she refused to get her tubes tied)
and this time the baby
came out healthy,
but some lady from the state
took the baby away
because of her history.
She went to court like a hundred
times to get her baby back.
She finally won custody
but two weeks later she shows
up at my house at three in the morning

high as a kite,
says she can't
handle the baby,
it's raisin' Cain.
And so I took that kid like she was
my own,
and I read to her every night
just like I did with her mother,
and I'm telling you it
ain't gonna matter,
and you'd have to be pretty
fucking god damned stupid
to think so."

DEVOTEE

A fortyish white guy in a cheap suit
gets off the Greyhound bus,
climbs into my cab
and hisses, "The Raddison."
As I drive I try to talk to him
but he ignores me.
When I pull up to the Raddison
I read the marquee:
DALAI LAMA TO SPEAK TONIGHT.
"Here to see the Dolly Lama?" I say.
"Mm, hmm," he says
as if there would be no
other reason to be
in this lame town.
He snatches every cent of his change
like a monkey at a handfull
of peanuts
and swings his bag
violently from the trunk.
The bellhop gets the same "lesson by example"
as the man gives him
the cold shoulder
and turns and stomps away
through the hotel's glass doors
nearly knocking over a little
old lady
in a skullcap.

SOMETIMES A CABBY

Sometimes a cabby
makes a dozen trips in a row
from the resort on the hill
all the way out
to the airport,
counting money and burning rubber
on each return,
making plans for the
future, singing with the radio, everything
sunny, time to get in
shape, write your
mother a letter,
become a better, happier
human being,
maybe even fall in
love.
And sometimes a cabby
sits all day
broke and shivering
in an unmoving queue
at the Greyhound
bus station,
and smokes.

DROP TOWER

At the county fair
my wife Josie wanted to go
on the ride you could see
from a mile away,
so the carny strapped us
into our escape pod seats
and lifted us a hundred feet into the air
along a cylinder of rainbows.
At the top we were dolls in the fist
of a child about to sneeze,
legs dangling in the funnel cake air
when the world dropped out and
we found free fall
like children being tickled
to death.
The downward momentum
caused an unfamiliar burn
in my prostate
amid the five seconds of screaming.
Once again safe on the platform
I unbuckled to the mechanical music
but my smile
was a flat worm in the sun.
Now here we are
a year later,
Josie and I,
going down from the 10th floor
in this hospital elevator.
I still see the disappointment in her eyes
when she saw I was afraid
of a child's ride.
She holds my hand
tight as a rescue worker
as the cable lowers us
in this black box
smelling of urine
to another pure white hallway.

THE MEASLY SUBTRACTION

Cab drivers will lie about anything,
especially money.
"I made two grand last
week."
As if this explains
the holes in their
shoes,
the fact that they can't afford
a razor
and have breath like
a maggoty rhinoceros.
I always wonder why it is so important
to impress the rest,
when we all have
to go home alone
and count our greasy bills
and do the measly subtraction
of rent and electricity
and food and beer.
They lie and lie and the
world goes round
like godless miles through
the city
only to end up back
in the same hole.
We all want to be respected
even by those we do not respect
and even those who nobody respects
want the same thing and
feel the same pull,
the same question
of the self:
what will
my brother
think?

LORD OF THE WASPS

Wasps swarm around his trailer door
as he walks through them into
the sun
an old man lugging an oxygen tank
through the sand.
The tank goes "pssst, pssst, pssst..."
like it wants to tell him
a secret.
He walks like a creature from another world
with those hoses to his nose
sickly pale and spotted
with tired gray eyes.
He smoked five packs a day for years
working seventy hours a week
supporting his wife and three kids.
Finally when the last one
graduated from high school
he quit smoking.
He decided he wanted to live to
see his grandchildren.
Ten years after the last cigarette
the chest problems came.
He lives out in the desert now
in a beat up trailer
alone, not a drop of natural living water
for miles, wife dead
and all his family scattered
like cough spray across the country.
He has three grandchildren he's never met
and six months to live.
He sits outside the trailer every night
on a lawn chair
while the wasps sleep,
just a few crickets,
and his oxygen tank going "pssst,
                    pssst,
                            pssst..."

THREE LANES OF HELL

I'm sitting in my cab
stalled like a walrus
in rush hour,

filtering Friday fumes
through untrimmed nostril hairs,
watching two nuns argue in the Prelude

in my rearview mirror.
One of them flails her arms
like a black windmill around a face

twisted with hatred
like a g-force.
The other white knuckles

the wheel
and looks straight
into my eyes.

FLANK STEAK MY ASS

A middle-aged couple gets in my cab
at the cheapo hotel.
They want me to take them to a restaurant.

Make it someplace good, the man says.

I take them to El Corral.
Later they call for a ride back.

Let me ask you something, the man
says to me.
What is the signature steak in
Arizona?

I might have to think about that one
I say.

I'm from South Carolina, he says,
and the rib-eye is
our signature steak.

His woman nods in agreement.

We had a rib-eye back at that restaurant
he says
and it was not near
as good as the rib-eyes back home.

I'm not sure we have
a signature steak, I say,
we just like all kinds
around here, I guess.

That's weird, he says,
every place has a signature steak, I hope
it's not rib-eye
because that was not a very
good rib-eye back there.

Maybe flank steak? I say,
the Mexicans use a lot of flank steak for
carne asada and that's
a local popular dish.

Flank steak? he says.

Well, I say, I'm not an
expert.

Hear that Hon? he says.
Flank steak!
Flank steak my ass!

At the hotel
I drop them at the door
with 101 branded on it
and he gets out and
follows his wife's
chuckling haunches inside, shaking
his head at my stupidity.

THE DRAG

I hate to get up in the morning
to the alarm clock
to go out there
in the 113 degree heat
and try to make a little money.
Normal life is such a drag
with no diamonds in your
veins
no magic in your blood
and my girlfriend told me
she has never heard
a cat purr
and I thought,
I love you,
I love you,
but will it
be enough?

THE ENVELOPE WITH THE BIG RED STAMP

I got a letter from a guy in prison.
The envelope had a big
red stamp on it.
The guy had read a few of my poems in a
magazine.
In one poem I had used some swear words
and he didn't approve of that
while another poem was about sex
which was ok
as long as I didn't use the swear words.

He told me
he'd murdered his wife
and that he also wrote poetry
and he included several handwritten poems
in a tiny, beautiful
penmanship.
He said he believed in self-determinism
and wanted to know how
I felt about the improvement of
humanity.
He said prison had freed him
from responsibilities like keeping
himself fed and housed in an expensive
and insane society
and had given him time
to read and to figure
things out.
I wrote him back telling him I didn't
like his poems
(they were robotic)
and that I also had bars on my window
and worked 50 hours a week to
hold it together

and I told him I was not interested in
self-determinism or his
plans for humanity.
I told him if he wanted to save the world
he probably should have started
by not killing his wife,
which was a cruel thing
to say maybe,
but then again maybe you should ask his
wife's family before you
judge me.

I have wanted to murder many
times but never did.
Maybe that makes me a coward,
it's hard
to be sure about anything,
and anyway
he never wrote
back.

STACY AND THE RENEGADE

Stacy was a nurse
but she got caught stealing drugs
and the DEA took her out
in handcuffs,
little Stacy five foot nothin'.
She was inside
for two years
lost her nursing license
and that's why she's driving a cab.
Stacy isn't an
aberration—
around here everybody
is nuts.
Stacy is a day driver
and her partner who drives nights
is Kyle.
Kyle used to be a professional wrestler
named the Renegade
and he makes Stacy
look
like a saint.

WEDNESDAY NIGHT AT THE SURLY WENCH

With a crash two dykes came out
of the gay bar.
The big one had a knife
but the small one was fast and
made it to my cab
and ordered me to get hell movin'.
Before I could turn the key
the big one reached in and grabbed
the small one's arm and a large portion
of her hair and told me not to
move one fucking inch. The small one
managed to squirm free
and began running around the cab.
I shut and locked all the doors.
For a while the chase held
ground around the cab
with the big one cussing like a sailor
and the small one rubbing her greasy
hands all over my windows.
I started the engine
when I'd had enough.
I palmed the horn and pulled forward slowly
kind of bumping the fat one
in the belt.
Then I watched them in the rear view:
they walked toward each other
and embraced and then
kissed
before both giving
me the finger.
They went back into the
noisy bar
and I drove out
to the airport
to watch the
planes come in.

THE MERGE

A man in a big white truck with a
shredded-from-the-wind American flag flipping
flaps his gums cursing
in my rear view mirror.
I can't hear him but I see his face
distort and turn red
like an angry fish sunk
in a pissed-in tank.
As two lanes merge to one
a woman in a blue car on my right
tries to get in between
white truck and me,
following the huge yellow arrows
painted on the road,
and white truck speeds
faster toward my bumper
like a bratty child in line
for firecrackers.
The woman is persistent,
no spring pup but still unable
to imagine her own death,
until she finally shoe-horns
in inches away from a well-
paved death.
How no bumpers
touch or snarl together is
a miracle.
White truck blasts her with his dinosaur scream
but I don't look at him now,
instead I look at a pretty smile
utterly uncontaminated
by thought.

DOUBLETREE LIZ

She's sixty-one
and from Yuma
but lives in Tucson now,
moved here alone too many
summers ago
and got hired at the Doubletree Inn
on the switchboard.
She lights up
forty cigarettes a day
and wheezes from the ten ghost-like paces
from her apartment door
to my cab.
I say good morning
but she only puts a finger up in front of her
cross-hatched agony
and rolls her gravelly mucous
up the hill
to the back of her mouth.
She can never talk
until we get a mile
or more down Wilmot
towards the Doubletree
where construction makes it
stop and go, where between
movable parts of gloved workmen
kettles of tar boil and
stink at ten a.m.
If she's able
Liz tells me
schoolmarm tales
of a world clogged with bile
and privilege.
If I'm able
I wave her money away
like smoke.

MONSOON

The sky is an inkblot, the radio just a bit
of static ushering in each thunderbolt.

The dust in the streets grows legs
like the devil's puppies chasing their tails.

Suddenly it's as if God snaps
a wet rug an acre wide

and an iron rain stampedes across the roof.
I can do nothing but think of you.

Afterwards a song jumps back
on the radio in mid-chorus

and miles to the north, in the mountains,
the rivers begin to roar.

Acknowledgments

Some of these poems appered in: *New York Quarterly, My Favorite Bullet, 5 A.M., Sage Trail, Nerve Cowboy, Cokefish, Quercus, American Dissident, Chiron, Clark Street, Gutter Eloquence, Slipstream, Hanging Loose, The Laughing Dog, The Silt Reader, River King, Fight These Bastards, Sow's Ear, Raleigh Review, Main Street Rag, Abbey, Rattle, Zygote In My Coffee, Full of Crow, Poetry Warrior, Commonline, Underground Voices, Camel Saloon, Literary Burlesque, Horror, Sleaze & Trash, Orange Room Review, Clutching at Straws.*

Mather Schneider was born in 1970 in Peoria, Illinois. He has since lived in Arkansas, Washington State and currently Tucson, Arizona where he drives a cab. He has published hundreds of poems and stories in the small press since 1994. This is his second full-length book of poetry.

About NYQ Books™

NYQ Books™ was established in 2009 as an imprint of The New York Quarterly Foundation, Inc. Its mission is to augment the *New York Quarterly* poetry magazine by providing an additional venue for poets already published in the magazine. A lifelong dream of NYQ's founding editor, William Packard, NYQ Books™ has been made possible by both growing foundation support and new technology that was not available during William Packard's lifetime. We are proud to present these books to you and hope that you will continue to support The New York Quarterly Foundation, Inc. and our poets and that you will enjoy these other titles from NYQ Books™:

Barbara Blatner	*The Still Position*
Amanda J. Bradley	*Hints and Allegations*
rd coleman	*beach tracks*
Joanna Crispi	*Soldier in the Grass*
Ira Joe Fisher	*Songs from an Earlier Century*
Sanford Fraser	*Tourist*
Tony Gloeggler	*The Last Lie*
Ted Jonathan	*Bones & Jokes*
Richard Kostelanetz	*Recircuits*
Iris Lee	*Urban Bird Life*
Kevin Pilkington	*In the Eyes of a Dog*
Jim Reese	*ghost on 3rd*
F. D. Reeve	*The Puzzle Master and Other Poems*
Jackie Sheeler	*Earthquake Came to Harlem*
Jayne Lyn Stahl	*Riding with Destiny*
Shelley Stenhouse	*Impunity*
Tim Suermondt	*Just Beautiful*
Douglas Treem	*Everything So Seriously*
Oren Wagner	*Voluptuous Gloom*
Joe Weil	*The Plumber's Apprentice*
Pui Ying Wong	*Yellow Plum Season*
Fred Yannantuono	*A Boilermaker for the Lady*
Grace Zabriskie	*Poems*

Please visit our website for these and other titles:

www.nyqbooks.org

www.ingramcontent.com/pod-product-compliance
Lightning Source LLC
LaVergne TN
LVHW011426080426
835512LV00005B/283